VOCAL DUET

CHRISTIAN WEDDING DUETS

ISBN 0-7935-9369-7

HAL•LEONARD®
CORPORATION
7777 W. BLUEMOUND RD. P.O. BOX 13819 MILWAUKEE, WI 53213

Visit Hal Leonard Online at
www.halleonard.com

VOCAL DUET
CHRISTIAN WEDDING DUETS

CONTENTS

All I Long For

Recorded by Susan Ashton & Michael English

Words and Music by
CHARLIE PEACOCK

HE-1st time
SHE-2nd time
SHE-3rd time

Here I ___

(the male may improvise during the female verses)

am, teach me ___ true,

*Note: This is basically the arrangement recorded by Susan Ashton and Michael English,
but the vocal parts have been adapted for a live duet performance.*

Butterfly Kisses

Recorded by Bob Carlisle

Words and Music by RANDY THOMAS
and BOB CARLISLE

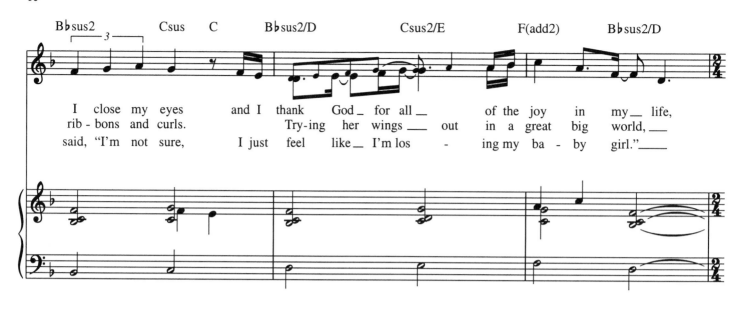

I close my eyes and I thank God for all of the joy in my life,
rib - bons and curls. Try-ing her wings out in a great big world,
said, "I'm not sure, I just feel like I'm los - ing my ba - by girl."

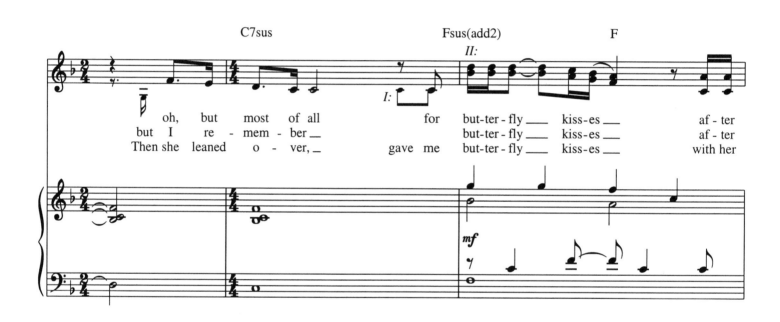

oh, but most of all for but-ter-fly kiss-es af - ter
but I re - mem - ber for but-ter-fly kiss-es af - ter
Then she leaned o - ver, gave me but-ter-fly kiss-es with her

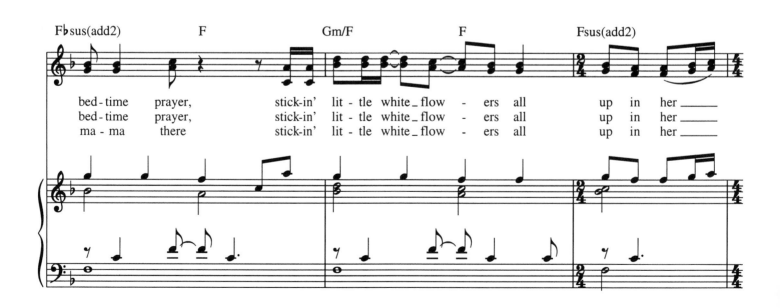

bed - time prayer, stick-in' lit - tle white flow - ers all up in her
bed - time prayer, stick-in' lit - tle white flow - ers all up in her
ma - ma there stick-in' lit - tle white flow - ers all up in her

Cherish the Treasure

Recorded by Steve Green

Words and Music by
JON MOHR

Moderately, gently

Male Solo: I cher - ish the treas - ure, the

treas - ure of you. Life - long com - pan - ion, I

give my - self to you. God has en - a - bled me to ___

How Beautiful

Recorded by Twila Paris

Words and Music by
TWILA PARIS

Commitment Song

Recorded by Chris & Diane Machen

Words and Music by ROBERT STERLING
and CHRIS MACHEN

God Causes All Things to Grow

Recorded by Steve Green

Words and Music by STEVEN CURTIS CHAPMAN
and STEVE GREEN

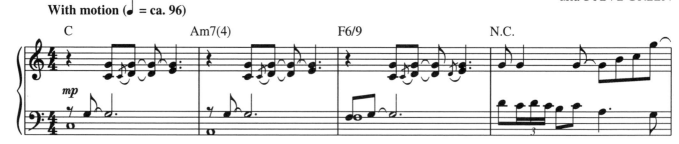

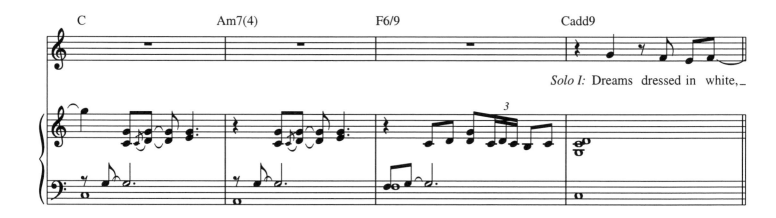

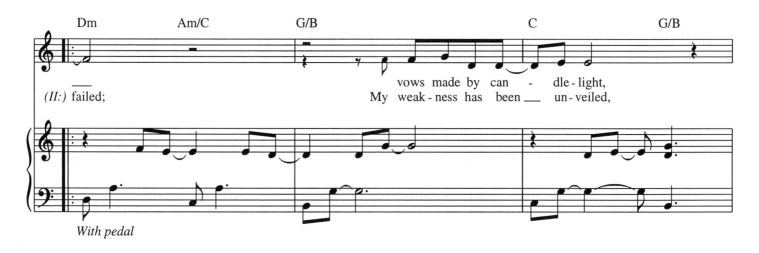

Through ev-'ry sea - son we know_ He will guard_ the life_ that He's

plant- ed in_ our souls._ And when we feel the cold_ winds blow, we'll

hold to what_ we know: God caus- es all things_ to grow._

—

Solo II: You know where I've

Household of Faith

Recorded by Steve & Marijean Green

Words by BRENT LAMB
Music by JOHN ROSASCO

I Will Be Here

Recorded by Steven Curtis Chapman

Words and Music by
STEVEN CURTIS CHAPMAN

Solo I: To-mor-row morn-in' if you __ wake up and the sun does __ not __ ap-pear,

Solo II: To-mor-row morn-in' if you __ wake up and the fu-ture is __ un-clear,__

- er, ___ 'cause I will be here. ___

A♭2(no3rd)   E♭2   A♭2(no3rd)   **D.S. al Coda**

CODA   E♭   B♭/D   Cm   Cm7/B♭   E♭/F   F7

I will be here ___ and you can cry on ___ my shoul-

B♭   B♭maj7/A   E♭maj7/G   A♭   E♭/G

- der   when the mir - ror tells ___ us we're old - er.   I ___ will hold ___

The Lord's Prayer

By ALBERT HAY MALOTTE

I.O.U. Me

Recorded by BeBe & CeCe Winans

Words and Music by BEBE WINANS, BILLY SPRAGUE,
KEITH THOMAS, THOMAS HEMBY and MIKE RAPP

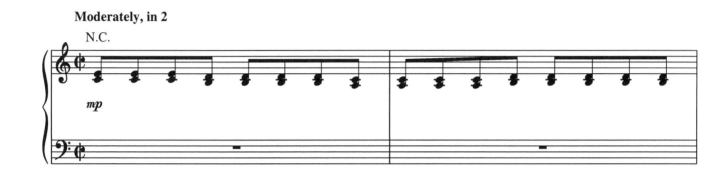

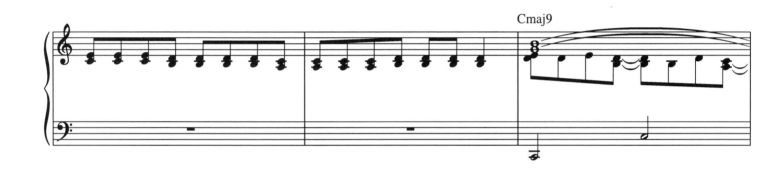

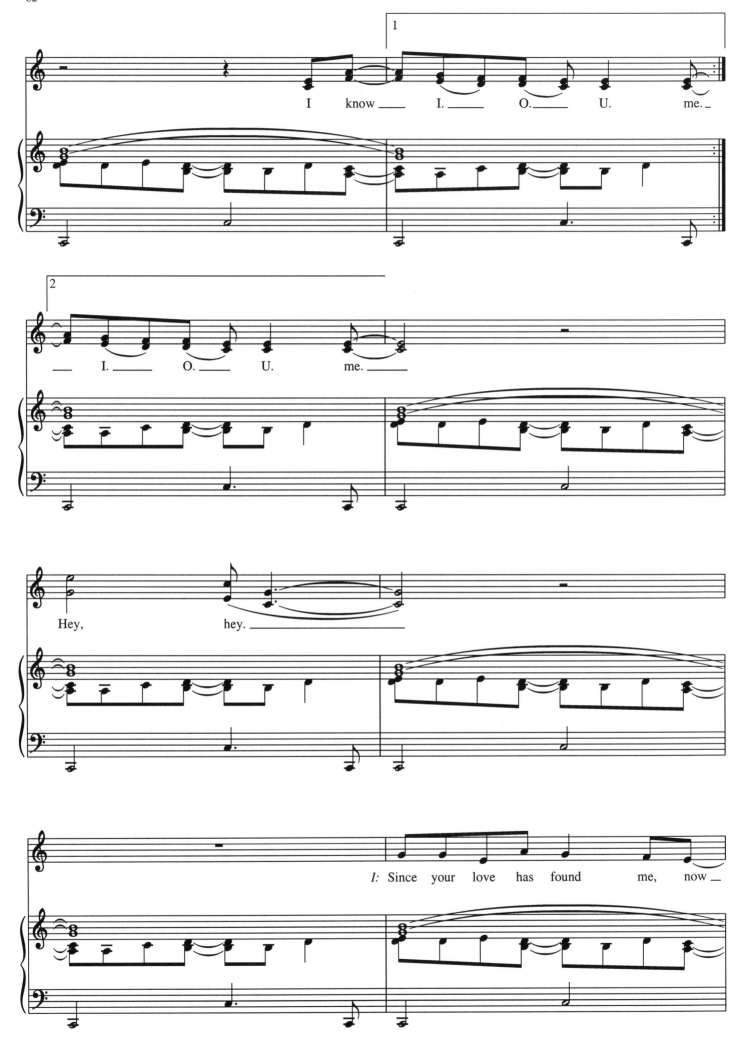

Lost Without You

Recorded by BeBe & CeCe Winans

Words and Music by BEBE WINANS
and KEITH THOMAS

Love of the Lasting Kind

Words and Music by CLAIRE CLONINGER
and DON CASON

Love Will Be Our Home

Recorded by Sandi Patty

Words and Music by
STEVEN CURTIS CHAPMAN

Love will be ___ our home.

Wher - ev - er there ___ are chil - dren sing - ing,

where a ten - der heart _____ is beat - ing;

We can live ___ to - geth - er there, ___ 'cause love will be ___ our

home. _____

I: With

* The ending either could be done loud or soft.

Love's Not a Feeling

Recorded by Steve Camp

Words and Music by STEVE CAMP
and ROB FRAZIER

Light Rock tempo

HE: Take a look a - round,___ so man-y bro - ken hearts on the ground.___
(HE:) love that Je - sus showed___ and our des - perate hearts need it so.___

___ No one was there ___ to take the time___
___ His love is a - live, ___ it nev - er ends,___

___ to real - ly care.___ *SHE:* Well, a com - mit-ment's what love should___ be;
___ it nev - er dies.___ *SHE:* God won't walk out on us

Repeat on D.S. only

lose or throw a - way. ___ Lord, give us the cour - age to live ___ it ev - 'ry day. _____

To Coda

HE: There's a

(ad lib. Sax solo)

Only God Could Love You More

Words and Music by DWIGHT LILES
and NILES BOROP

Moderately fast, tenderly

I asked the Lord _ for some - one,_ and I al - ways knew_
I'm tempt-ed to _ be say - ing_ that we met _ by chance,_

that in God's time and in God's way _ it would
but God was there at ev - 'ry turn, _ in

be some-one like you. _____
ev - 'ry cir-cum - stance. _____

All my hopes and
To share this life God

Perfect Union

Words and Music by JOHN ANDREW SCHREINER
and MATTHEW WARD

Solo I: There's a love ___ that lasts ___ a life-
Solo II: And there are times ___ in ev-'ry un-

- time,   love be-tween ___ a man ___ and
- ion   when hard times ___ and trou-ble

wife. _____   Love so strong ___ it goes ___ be-yond ___ our rea - son.
fall, _____   tear-ing at ___ the seams ___ of ___ love, _____

Seekers of Your Heart

Recorded by Larnelle Harris

Words and Music by MELODIE TUNNEY,
DICK TUNNEY and BEVERLY DARNALL

This Very Day

Recorded by Paul Overstreet

Words and Music by JOHN ELLIOTT
and PAUL OVERSTREET

HE: I've been search - ing all __ my life __ for the wom - an I __ was meant __ to make __ my __ wife.

HE: Like the an - swer to __ my prayers, __ from this day on __ I'll wake __ to find __ her __ there.

SHE: And

and I will face each ris - ing sun_ nev - er

end - ing what's_ be - gun_ this ver - y day. _

To Have and to Hold

Words and Music by
ROY E. BRONKEMA

Wedding Prayer

Words and Music by
MARY RICE HOPKINS

Gently in four ♩ = 82

Solo I: Lord, _____ take our lives _____ As two who love You _ join as one. _

Solo II: Fa - ther, _____ You are love _ From the be - gin - ning of time. _

_ And let our love grow _ as Your love _

_ You made us to join _____ as

_ grows in us, Bind us to - geth - er so we

man and _ wife, To live to - geth - er, the Cre -

Wedding
COLLECTIONS FOR VOICE
From Hal Leonard

THE SINGER'S WEDDING ANTHOLOGY

An unprecedented, comprehensive look at wedding repertoire. Rather than just one style of music, like most wedding collections for voice, we have included classical and traditional material, popular songs, and contemporary Christian music. The anthology is available in 3 versions: High Voice, Low Voice, and Duets. The two solo volumes (High and Low) contain the same 45 selections, but in appropriate keys to high or low voices. Includes: I Swear • Just the Way You Are • When I Fall in Love • Someone Like You • The Language of Jesus Is Love • God Causes All Things to Grow • I Will Be Here • Ave Maria • Bist Du Bei Mir • Entreat Me Not to Leave Thee • Panis Angelicus • Whither Thou Goest • and many others. The duet collection contains 25 songs, including: Up Where We Belong • All I Ask of You • Endless Love • Let It Be Me • Household of Faith • Jesu Joy of Man's Desiring • Panis Angelicus • and many others.

00740006	High Voice	$19.95
00740008	Low Voice	$19.95
00740005	Duets	$14.95

WEDDING CLASSICS

The definitive collection of 12 classical and traditional favorites for the wedding service, packaged with an excellent recording of full performances (featuring top quality young singers) and accompaniments only. Contents: Bist du Bei Mir (Bach) • Entreat Me Not to Leave Thee (Gounod) • Because, Wher'er You Walk (Handel) • Oh Promise Me, Ich Liebe Dich (Grieg) • Ave Maria (Schubert) • Ave Maria (Bach/Gounod) • Du Ring An Meinem Finger (Schumann) • Widmung (Schumann) • I Love You Truly, Pur Ti Miro (Monteverdi – duet).

| 00740053 | High Voice Book/CD package | $17.95 |
| 00740054 | Low Voice Book/CD package | $17.95 |

10 POPULAR WEDDING DUETS

with a companion CD

10 duets for the wedding. The companion CD contains two performances of each song, one with singers, the other is the orchestrated instrumental track for accompaniment. Contents: All I Ask of You • Annie's Song • Don't Know Much • Endless Love • I Swear • In My Life • Let It Be Me • True Love • Up Where We Belong • When I Fall in Love.

00740002 Book/CD package *$19.95*

10 WEDDING SOLOS

with a companion CD

A terrific, useful collection of 10 songs for the wedding, including both popular songs and contemporary Christian material. There are two versions of each song on the companion CD, first with full performances with singers, then with the instrumental accompaniments only. Contents: Here, There and Everywhere • I Swear • The Promise • Someone Like You • Starting Here Starting Now • God Causes All Things to Grow • Parent's Prayer • This Is the Day • Wedding Prayer • Where There Is Love.

00740004 High Voice Book/CD package *$19.95*
00740009 Low Voice Book/CD package *$19.95*

12 WEDDING SONGS

arranged for medium voice and fingerstyle guitar

A practical collection of music chosen particularly for the wedding, in new arrangements designed to flatter voice with guitar accompaniment. The collection combines classical/traditional and popular selections. The guitar part is presented in both standard notation and tablature. Contents: Annie's Song • Ave Maria (Schubert) • The First Time Ever I Saw Your Face • Here, There and Everywhere • I Swear • If • In My Life • Jesu, Joy of Man's Desiring • Let It Be Me • Unchained Melody • When I Fall in Love • You Needed Me.

00740007 . . . . *$12.95*

SINGER'S CHRISTIAN WEDDING COLLECTION

30 songs, including: Butterfly Kisses • Cherish the Treasure • Commitment Song • Household of Faith • How Beautiful • I Will Be Here • Lost Without You • Love Will Be Our Home • Parent's Prayer (Let Go of Two) • This Is the Day (A Wedding Song) • and more.

| 00740108 | High Voice | $19.95 |
| 00740109 | Low Voice | $19.95 |

FOR MORE INFORMATION, SEE YOUR LOCAL MUSIC DEALER,
OR WRITE TO:

HAL•LEONARD®
CORPORATION

7777 W. BLUEMOUND RD. P.O. BOX 13819 MILWAUKEE, WI 53213

Prices, contents and availability subject to change without notice. Some products may not be available outside the U.S.A.

The Most Romantic Music In The World

The Best Love Songs Ever
65 all-time favorites, including: Always • Anniversary Song • Beautiful In My Eyes • Can't Help Falling In Love • Can You Feel the Love Tonight • Could I Have This Dance • Don't Know Much • Endless Love • Have I Told You Lately • How Deep Is Your Love • I.O.U. • Just The Way You Are • Longer • Love Me Tender • Misty • Saving All My Love For You • She Believes In Me • Sunrise, Sunset • Try To Remember • Vision Of Love • When I Fall In Love • You Needed Me • Your Song.
00359198 ....$17.95

The Big Book Of Love And Wedding Songs
81 romantic classics, contemporary favorites, and sacred standards in one convenient collection, including: All I Ask Of You • Anniversary Song • Ave Maria • Could I Have This Dance • Endless Love • Forever And Ever, Amen • Longer • Lost In Your Eyes • Sunrise, Sunset • You Decorated My Life • and more.
00311567 ....$19.95

Contemporary Christian Wedding Songbook
30 appropriate songs for weddings, including: Household Of Faith • Love In Any Language • Love Will Be Our Home • Parents' Prayer • This Is Love • Where There Is Love • and more.
00310022 ....$14.95

The Definitive Love Collection
Over 100 sentimental favorites in one collection! Includes: All I Ask Of You • Can't Help Falling In Love • (They Long To Be) Close To You • Endless Love • The Glory Of Love • Have I Told You Lately That I Love You • Here And Now • I've Got My Love To Keep Me Warm • Isn't It Romantic? • It Could Happen To You • Let's Fall In Love • Love Me Tender • Save The Best For Last • So In Love • Somewhere Out There • A Time For Us • Unforgettable • When I Fall In Love • A Whole New World (Aladdin's Theme) • and more.
00311681 ....$29.95

Contemporary Wedding & Love Songs
21 romantic hits of the '80s and '90s, including: All I Ask of You • Always • Beautiful in My Eyes • Endless Love • Have I Told You Lately • Save the Best for Last • When You Say Nothing at All • A Whole New World • You Must Love Me • more.
00310283 P/V/G $12.95

The New Complete Wedding Songbook
41 of the most requested and beloved songs for romance and weddings. Features: And This Is My Beloved • Anniversary Song • The Anniversary Waltz • Ave Maria • Can't Help Falling In Love • Canon in D (Pachelbel) • Could I Have This Dance • Endless Love • Feelings • For All We Know • The Hawaiian Wedding Song • How Deep Is Your Love • I Just Fall In Love Again • I Love You Truly • If We Only Have Love • Just The Way You Are • Let Me Call You Sweetheart • Longer • The Lord's Prayer • Love Me Tender • Love's Grown Deep • Melody of Love • Sunrise, Sunset • Through The Years • Too Much Heaven • True Love • Try To Remember • When I Need You • Whither Thou Goest • You Needed Me • You're My Everything • Your Song • and more.
00309326 ....$12.95

Isn't It Romantic?
A Treasury Of Classic Love Songs
50 romantic favorites, including: All The Things You Are • Body And Soul • If Ever I Would Leave You • Isn't It Romantic? • Misty • My Romance • The Nearness Of You • Smoke Gets In Your Eyes • The Very Thought Of You • and more.
00310009 ....$14.95

New Ultimate Love & Wedding Songbook
90 songs, including: And I Love Her • Could I Have This Dance• Endless Love • Here, There And Everywhere • Just The Way You Are • Longer • Misty • One Hand, One Heart • Somewhere • Sunrise, Sunset • Through The Years • You Needed Me • more.
00361445 ....$19.95

Songs Of Love
58 romantic ballads, including: All The Things You Are • Can You Feel The Love Tonight • A Fine Romance • Friends & Lovers • Have I Told You Lately • I Swear • Misty • The Power Of Love • Saving All My Love For You • Truly • When I Fall In Love • A Whole New World • and more.
00311704 ....$15.95

Songs Of Romance
35 romantic favorites, including: All I Ask Of You • And I Love Her • Can't Smile Without You • Could I Have This Dance • Don't Know Much • Endless Love • Feelings • Forever And Ever Amen • Hopelessly Devoted To You • How Am I Supposed To Live Without You • How Deep Is Your Love • Imagine • I'll Be Loving You (Forever) • Just The Way You Are • Longer • Sometimes When We Touch • Somewhere Out There • You Decorated My Life • more.
00490361 ....$12.95

Wedding Songs Country Style
30 songs, including: Always On My Mind • Could I Have This Dance • Forever And Ever, Amen • The Keeper Of The Stars • Love Can Build a Bridge • +Love Me Tender • One Boy, One Girl • Through The Years • and more.
00310183 ....$12.95

Wedding Songs Of Love & Friendship
28 love songs appropriate for use in Christian services. Features: Always • Doubly Good To You • Let Us Climb The Hill Together • Longer • The Lord's Prayer • Sunrise, Sunset • Wedding Prayer • What A Difference You've Made In My Life.
00361489 ....$10.95